Risk Management Framework 2.0 Workbook

James Broad

Emily Leinenbach, Technical Editor

Cyber-Recon Publishing
Cyber-Recon, LLC

This book is dedicated to you, the lifelong learner. The person who is always looking to expand your knowledge and skillset. The one that good enough is never good enough. Keep learning and growing, keep contributing to the computer security and risk management field.

"Risk management is a more realistic term than safety. It implies that hazards are ever-present, that they must be identified, analyzed, evaluated and controlled or rationally accepted."

-Jerome F. Lederer

Introduction

Introduction to the Risk Management Framework 2.0 (RMF 2.0) and the (ISC)^2®

Certified Authorization Professional (CAP)® certification workbook.

The Risk Management Framework (RMF) was introduced to standardize system risk management and aligns with the organizational or enterprise-wide risk management program.
The RMF leverages applying security and privacy controls at the system level and assessing their functionality in not only protecting the information system but also protecting the organization or enterprise. The framework determines the risk the system will introduce to the organization if placed into production.

Initially, the RMF met with various acceptance levels; however, once organizations realized the savings, improved security, and compliance, its acceptance grew substantially. This acceptance was not only within the government but also in private industries that were not mandated to use the RMF but realized the benefits of this process. Now you will see public and private organizations capitalizing on the benefits of the RMF.

The National Institute of Standards and Technology (NIST) updated the RMF to be more effective and comprehensive. One of the significant components of this update was the addition of the Prepare step.
This step contains two different phases, organizational preparation and system prepare. This updated RMF, often referred to as RMF 2.0, also moved, consolidated, and added tasks in the existing steps. NIST also removed the numbering scheme prevalent in RMF 1.0, replacing it with alphabetic characters. The final major update was aligning the RMF with the NIST Cyber Security Framework (CSF) where applicable.

This workbook walks through every step and task of RMF 2.0, asking the reader to review each task and answer the main points of each task. This allows the reader to ensure they fully understand all of the tasks of this updated process. Each task includes a QR code that links to a video discussing the task. The workbook is designed to reinforce the major and minor points of the tasks that make up RMF 2.0.

We look forward to you comments. Every effort has been made to ensure this workbook is correct, however if you do notice an error, please contact us at info@Cyber-Recon.com.

Table of Contents

4

How to use this Workbook

https://csrc.nist.gov/publications/detail/sp/800-37/rev-2/final

This workbook is intended to be an aid in the understanding and learning of the newest version of the Risk Management Framework – RMF 2.0. The workbook is designed to be used with the free downloadable version of NIST SP 800-37, the numerous linked videos, books on the RMF, or any combination of these resources.

For each of the major subjects, steps and tasks of RMF 2.0 an associated video is available to be viewed on YouTube. You can access the video by scanning the QR code with any modern cell phone or using the listed uniform resource locator (URL), more commonly known as webpage address. The author elected to post the videos on YouTube to ensure the widest availability and access.

It is suggested that NIST SP 800-37 R2 be downloaded from the link on this page for reference. You are welcome to use this workbook with this special publication of any of the books available on RMF from resources like Amazon. The videos serve to reenforce the learning when coupled with the workbook.

The workbook focuses on preparing individuals to implement the RMF but serves as an excellent resource for those seeking to take the (ISC)^2 ® CAP ® certification exam.

Introduction to the CAP

Acronyms

Define the following acronyms.

(ISC)^2: ____

CAP: ____

AO: ____

IT: ____

CBK: ____

CPE: ____

Fill in the blanks

1. Passing the CAP exam proved you have the knowledge and ability to:

   a. ____

   b. ____

   c. ____

2. Who can benefit from the CAP certification?

   a. ____

   b. ____

   c. ____

   d. ____

   e. ____

   f. ____

3. What are the requirements to obtain the CAP certification?

   a. ____

   b. ____

4. If you do not meet the requirements for the CAP what option do you have?

   a. ____

5. What are the requirements for that option?

    a. ____

6. Who can benefit from the CAP certification?

    a. ____

    b. ____

    c. ____

    d. ____

    e. ____

    f. ____

7. What DoD job levels are you qualified to work with the CAP certification?

    a. ____

    b. ____

8. Fill in the blanks on the following diagram to identify the steps of RMF 2.0

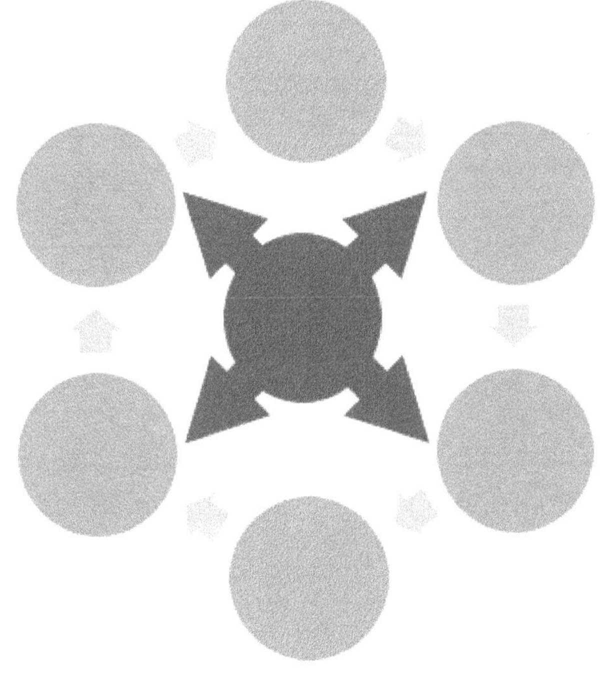

9. List some benefits of CAP certification

    a. ____

    b. ____

    c. ____

    d. ____

    e. ____

    f. ____

    g. ____

    h. ____

10. List some benefits of $(ISC)^2$ membership

    a. ____

    b. ____

    c. ____

    d. ____

    e. ____

    f. ____

    g. ____

    h. ____

    i. ____

    j. ____

    k. ____

    l. ____

11. What are the Domains of the CAP and percentage of the exam?

    a. ____

    b. ____

    c. ____

    d. ____

    e. ____

    f. ____

    g. ____

12. How many questions are on the CAP exam?

    a. ____

13. How much time is allowed for the exam?

    a. ____

14. What is the minimum score required to pass the exam?

    a. ____

15. What is the cost of the exam?

    a. ____

16. How long will you be certified once you pass the exam?

    a. ____

Notes:

____

____

____

____

____

____

____

____

____

____

____

____

____

____

____

____

RMF / CAP Careers

Acronyms

Define the following acronyms

IA: ____

ISSO: ____

ISSM: ____

CE: ____

NE:____

COOP: ____

CASP CE: ____

CISM: ____

CISSP: ____

GSLC: ____

CCNA (Security): ____

IAM: ____

Complete the following

1. The CAP certification will qualify a person for what roles in the DoD?

    a. ____

    b. ____

2. In the job categories listed above, what are some potential job titles?

    a. ____

    b. ____

    c. ____

    d. ____

    e. ____

    f. ____

    g. ____

3. What DoD role has functions such as apply IA policies and procedures, manage secure computing environments, and recognize and report possible security violations?

    a. ____

The following questions relate to the DoD role in question 3.

4. What is the experience level?

    a. ____

5. What knowledge should you have for these roles?

    a. ____

6. What certifications meet the requirements for these roles?

    a. ____

    b. ____

7. What DoD role has functions such as develop and implement IA policies, assist in gathering of evidence around computer crimes, and coordinate IA inspection and reviews?

    a. ____

7a. The following questions relate to the DoD role in question 7. What is the experience level?

    a. ____

8. What knowledge should you have for these roles?

    a. ____

9. What certifications meet the requirements for these roles?

    a. ____

    b. ____

    c. ____

    d. ____

    e. ____

    f. ____

Notes:

What is NIST?

Acronyms:

Define the following

NIST: ____

SP: ____

FIPS: ____

NISTIR: ____

ITL: ____

Complete the following

1. When was NIST founded?

    a. ____

2. NIST is part of what U.S. Department?

    a. ____

3. Provide information about SPs

    a. ____

    b. ____

    c. ____

    ____

4. What is special about the NIST SP 800 series?

    a. ____

    b. ____

5. Provide some information about FIPS documents.

a. ____

b. ____

c. ____

6. Provide some information about NISTIR documents,

a. ____

b. ____

7. Provide some information about ITL Bulletins.

a. ____

b. ____

c. ____

8. What other types of documents does NIST produce?

a. ____

b. ____

c. ____

d. ____

9.Where can you find more information about NIST publications?

a. ____

Notes:

____

____

____

____

____

____

Organization-Wide Risk Management

https://www.youtube.com/watch?v=LkTOGyC-K4k

NIST SP 800-37, 2.1

Acronyms

1. Define the following new terms

    a. SDLC: ____

Complete the following

2. Managing security and privacy risk involves the entire organization. Provide the activities for the following roles:

    c. Senior Leaders: _______________________________________

    d. Mid-Level: ____

    e. Individuals: ____

3. Managing risk impacts all of the organization including the following:

    b. ____

    c. ____

    d. ____

    e. ____

4. Fill in the blanks on the following Diagram

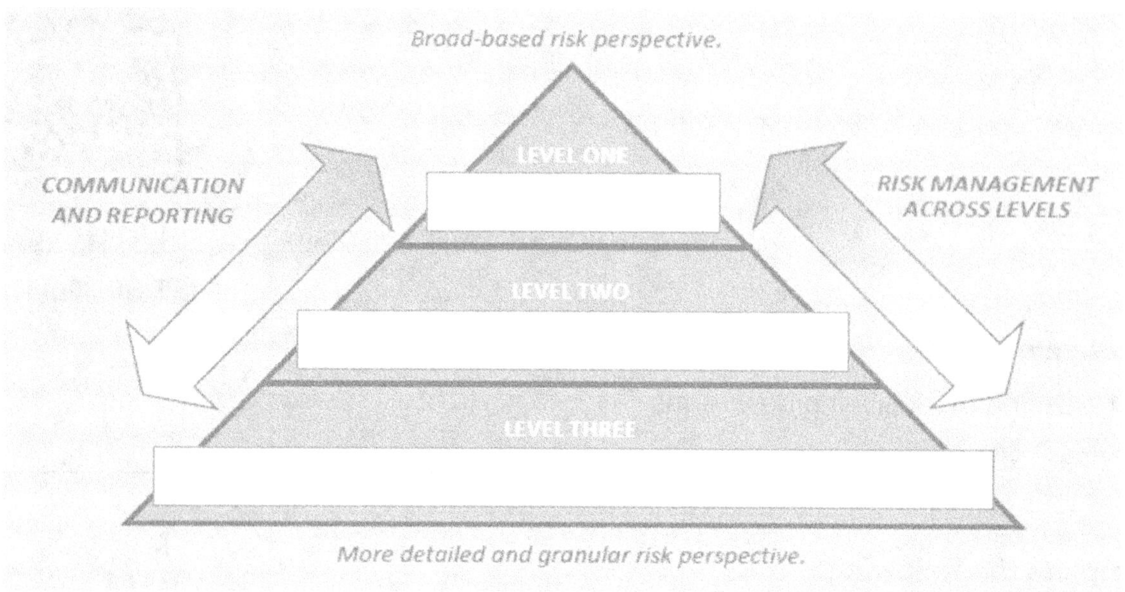

5. Risk based decisions at the system level are linked to:

   a. ____

   b. ____

   c. ____

      ____

   d. ____

      ____

6. List some important steps that the organization needs to complete to effectively launce the use of the RMF.

   a. ____

   b. ____

   c. ____

   d. ____

   e. ____

   f. ____

   g. ____

   h. ____

   i. ____

    j. ____

    k. ____

    l. ____

    m. ____

    n. ____

7. What activities are conducted at each Level

    a. Level 1: _______________________________

    b. Level 2: _______________________________

    c. Level 3: _______________________________

       Level 3: _______________________________

8. Controls are designated by the organization as system-specific, hybrid, or common (inherited) controls are done so in accordance with:

    a. ____

    b. ____

    c. ____

9. When are traceability concerns addressed at?

    a. ____

    b. ____

    c. ____

    d. ____

    e. ____

    f. ____

10. The iterative nature of the risk management process reenforces security and privacy risks are:

    a. ____

    b. ____

    c. ____

    d. ____

11. Without adequate risk management preparation at the organizational level, security and privacy activities can become:

    a. ____

    b. ____

    c. ____

12. A lack of adequate preparation by organizations could result in

    a. ____

    b. ____

Notes:____

____

____

____

____

____

____

____

____

____

____

____

____

____

____

____

____

____

RMF Steps and Structure

NIST SP 800-37, 2.2

Acronyms

1. Define the following new terms

   No new Acronyms are introduced in this topic

Complete the following

2. How many steps are in the RMF version 2.0?

   a. ____

3. List the steps of the RMF version 2.0

   a. ____

   b. ____

   c. ____

   d. ____

   e. ____

   f. ____

   g. ____

4. Name and describe the first step:

   a. ____

   ____

5. Name and describe the second step:

    a. ____

    ____

6. Name and describe the third step:

    a. ____

    ____

7. Name and describe the fourth step:

    a. ____

    ____

8. Name and describe the fifth step:

    a. ____

    ____

9. Name and describe the sixth step:

    a. ____

    ____

10. Name and describe the seventh step:

    a. ____

    ____

11. Fill in the missing information for the following diagram:

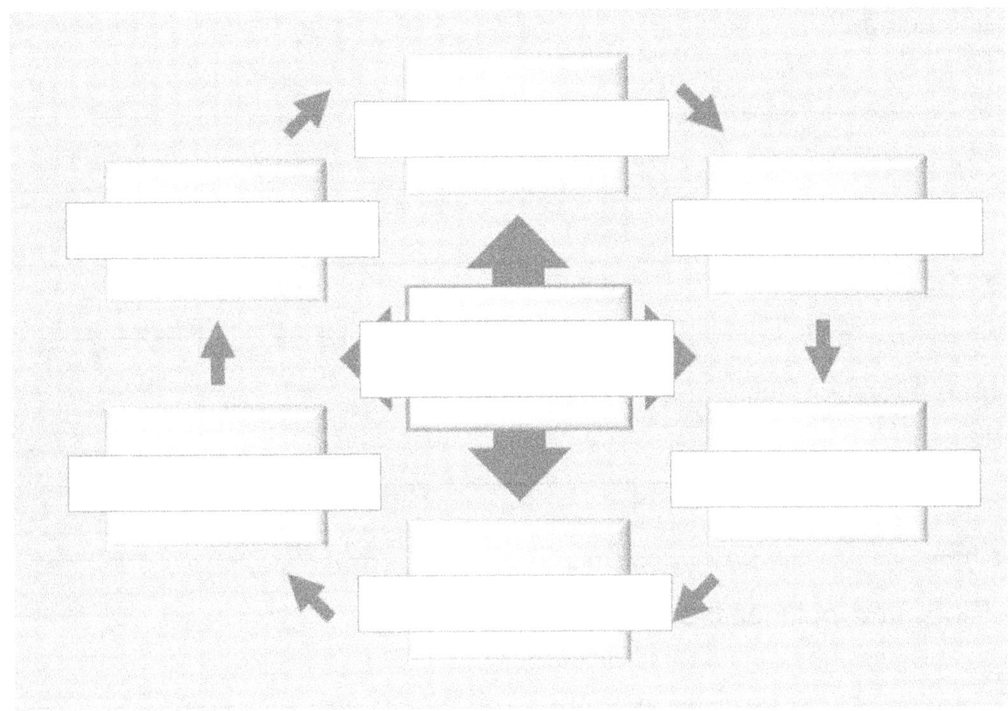

12. Is it required that the steps of the RMF be performed in order?

    a. ____

13. Can the RMF be modified by the organization?

    a. ____

14. Why would an organization or system change the order of the RMF steps?

    a. ____

15. Do all of the tasks in the RMF need to be completed?

    a. ____

16. Are there any tasks that do not need to be completed?

    a. ____

17. Organizations have flexibility in how the steps/tasks are carried out, what does this flexibility include?

    a. ____

    b. ____

    c. ____

    d. ____

18. Resource Allocation Includes:

    a. ____

    b. ____

19. Each RMF Step includes the following:

    a. ____

    b. ____

    c. ____

20. What areas of an organization can a step or task be carried out at?

    a. ____

    b. ____

    c. ____

21. Each task contains the following

    a. ____

    b. ____

    c. ____

    d. ____

    e. ____

    f. ____

Notes:

____

____

____

____

____

____

____

____

Information Security and Privacy in the RMF

NIST SP 800-37, 2.3

Acronyms

1. Define the following new acronyms

PII: ____

OMB: ____

Complete the following

2. OMB Circular A-130 establishes general policy for

a. ____

b. ____

c. ____

d. ____

3. OMB Circular A-130 covers

a. ____

b. ____

c. ____

d. ____

e. ____

f. ____

4. OMB Circular addresses

a. ____

b. ____

5. Privacy risks to PII may also result from other activities, including what types of activities?

    a. ____

    b. ____

    c. ____

6. What version of OMB Circular A-130 addresses PII?

    a. ____

7. Information security programs are responsible for protecting information and information systems from:

    a. ____

    b. ____

    c. ____

    d. ____

    e. ____

8. Information security programs provide protection to

    a. ____

    b. ____

    c. ____

9. Privacy programs are responsible for ensuring compliance with applicable privacy requirements and for managing the risks to individuals associated with:

    a. ____

    b. ____

    c. ____

    d. ____

    e. ____

    f. ____

    g. ____

    h. ____

    i. ____

    j. ____

10. Shared security and privacy responsibility require the two programs to collaborate on security controls when

    a. ____

    b. ____

    c. ____

    d. ____

11. Some PII protections are beyond the scope of information security for example

    a. ____

    b. ____

    c. ____

12. A privacy control can be defined as a number of high-level safeguards, what are these high-level safeguard categories?

    a. ____

    b. ____

    c. ____

13. What is a term for a control that addresses both security and privacy requirements?

    a. ____

14. What is a term for a control that addresses only security requirements?

    a. ____

15. What is a term for a control that addresses only privacy requirements?

    a. ____

16. The risk management processes described in the RMF is equally applicable to

    a. ____

Notes:

____

____

____

____

____

Systems and System Elements

https://youtu.be/dZlzSVb6Hx0

NIST SP 800-37, 2.4

Acronyms

1. Define the following new terms

    a. ISO:

    ____

Complete the following

2. What context should an information system be described in?

    a. ____

3. Systems Security Engineering should be viewed as part of what process:

    a. ____

4. According to ISO 15288, what is a system?

    a. ____

    ____

5. According to Federal Law Enforcement, what is a system?

    a. ____

    ____

6. Can system resources contain other resources?

    a. ____

7. What are some system elements?

    a. ____

    b. ____

    c. ____

8. How can requirements be implemented?

    a. ____

9. When talking about systems, what may satisfy stated system requirements?

    a. ____

10. Can interconnections allow a system to meet requirements?

    a. ____

11. What influences the system and its operations?

    a. ____

12. What does the authorization boundary define?

    a. ____

13. What is another term for authorization boundary?

    a. ____

14. What can an enabling system provide?

    a. ____

15. If a facility provides controls what are they called?

    a. ____

Notes:

Authorization Boundaries

NIST SP 800-37, 2.5

Acronyms

16. Define the following new acronyms

> No new acronyms are defined in this topic

Complete the following

17. What task in the RMF introduces Authorization Boundaries?

> a. ____

18. What does the Authorization Boundary establish?

> a. ____

19. What does the Authorization Boundary include?

> a. ____
>
> b. ____

20. What are the risks of making too large of an Authorization Boundary?

> a. ____

21. What are the risks of making too small of an Authorization Boundary?

> a. ____

22. What are some general guidelines for determining what constitutes an Authorization Boundary, in relation to management and budget?

> a. ____
>
> b. ____

23. What are some additional general guidelines for determining what constitutes an Authorization Boundary?

    a. ____

    b. ____

    c. ____

    d. ____

24. Is the Authorization Boundary ever reviewed, and if so, what is it part of?

    a. ____

25. What are some implications of selecting the Authorization Boundary?

    a. ____

    b. ____

    c. ____

    d. ____

    e. ____

26. What are some impacts of Authorization Boundary selection?

    a. ____

    b. ____

    c. ____

    d. ____

    e. ____

Notes:

____

____

____

____

____

____

____

____

____

Requirements and Controls

NIST SP 800-37, 2.6

Acronyms

1. Define the following new terms

    ISO: ____

Complete the following

2. What context should an information system be described in?

    a. ____

3. Systems Security Engineering should be viewed as part of what process:

    a. ____

4. According to ISO 15288, what is a system?

    a. ____

    ____

5. According to Federal Law Enforcement, what is a system?

    a. ____

    ____

6. Can system resources contain other resources?

    a. ____

7. What are some system elements?

    a. ____

    b. ____

    c. ____

8. How can requirements be implemented?

    a. ____

    b. ____

9. When talking about systems, what may satisfy stated system requirements?

    a. ____

10. Can interconnections allow a system to meet requirements?

    a. ____

11. What influences the system and its operations?

    a. ____

12. What does the authorization boundary define?

    a. ____

13. What is another term for authorization boundary?

    a. ____

14. What can an enabling system provide?

    a. ____

15. If a facility provides controls what are they called?

    a. ____

    b. ____

Notes:

____

____

____

____

____

____

____

____

____

____

____

____

____

Security and Privacy Posture

https://youtu.be/IL32Zx0hdoM

NIST SP 800-37, 2.7

Acronyms

1. Define the following new acronyms

    There are no new acronyms introduced in this topic

Complete the following

2. What is the purpose of the RMF?

    a.

    b.

3. What is a key aspect of risk-based decision making for AOs?

    a.

4. What does the security and privacy posture represent?

    a.

5. When is the security and privacy posture of information systems and organization determined?

    a.

6. How is the security and privacy posture of information systems and organization determined?

    a.

7. What do Authorizing Officials use the security and privacy posture to determine?

    a. ____

____

Notes:

Supply Chain Risk Management

https://www.youtube.com/watch?v=XQEuIg_t2Ew

NIST SP 800-37, 2.8

Acronyms

1. Define the following new acronyms

SCRM: ____

Complete the following

2. What are some examples of some ways relationships with external providers can be established?

a.

____

b.

____

c.

____

d.

____

3. Who is responsible and accountable for risks incurred when using SCRM?

a. ____

4. According to this topic what presents an increasing amount of risk to an organization?

a. ____

____

5. What are some examples of threat events that may increase organizational risk?

    a. ____

    b. ____

    c. ____

    d. ____

    e. ____

    f. ____

6. Can risks based on the same threat be different when used in a system or element (acceptable risk increase) and when common or extended (raised the risk to unacceptable level) across the organization?

    a. ____

7. Supply chain risks are often associated with what?

    a. ____

    ____

    ____

    ____

8. How do organizations address supply chain risks?

    a. ____

9. What do SCRM roles specify?

    a. ____

    b. ____

    c. ____

    d. ____

    e. ____

10. What documents require external providers handling federal information or operating systems on behalf of the federal government to meet the same security and privacy requirements as federal agencies?

    a. ____

    b. ____

11. What framework can be used to manage supply chain risk management?

    a. ____

12. What step in the framework defined in number 11, cannot be conducted by nonfederal external providers?

    a. ____

13. SCRM activities involve what?

    a. ____

    b. ____

    c. ____

    d. ____

14. Why would SCRM plans be tailored?

    a. ____

____

15. The determination that the risk from acquiring products, systems, or services from external providers is acceptable depends on what?

    a. ____

____

16. How is the degree of control is established?

    a. ____

17. Ultimately, the responsibility for responding to risks from the use of component products, systems, and services from external providers remains with who?

    a. ____

18. Who is a chain of trust established with?

    a. ____

19. The SCRM strategy at levels 1 and 2 can be documented where?

    a. ____

    b. ____

20. The SCRM strategy at level 3 can be documented where?

    a. ____

    b. ____

21. Where can someone find a SCRM Strategy template be found?

    a. ____

Notes:

____

____

____

____

____

____

____

____

____

Updates to the RMF

Acronyms

1. Define the following new acronyms

C-Suite: ____

Complete the following

1. The RMF emphasizes risk management by promoting the development of security and privacy capabilities into what?

a. ____

2. Implementing the RMF allows organizations to maintain what?

a. ____

b. ____

3. List some Benefits of using the RMF

a. ____

b. ____

c. ____

____

d. ____

e. ____

f. ____

g. ____

h. ____

4. List the names of the steps of RMF 2.0

    a. ____

    b. ____

    c. ____

    d. ____

    e. ____

    f. ____

    g. ____

5. What did RMF 2.0 integrate and include in this version?

    a. ____

    b. ____

6. What is one of the key changes to RMF 2.0?

    a. ____

7. What step in RMF 2.0 would you see common controls and organizationally-tailored baselines?

    a. ____

8. What does the decision Authorization to Use encourage?

    a. ____

9. What can automation increase?

    a. ____

    b. ____

    c. ____

10. What are the seven improvements to the RMF?

      a. ____

      b. ____

      c. ____

      d. ____

      e. ____

      f. ____

      g. ____

11. What was important in the change to the title for SP 800-37 R2?

      a. ____

      b. ____

Notes:

____

____

____

____

____

____

____

____

____

____

____

____

____

____

____

____

____

____

Introduction to Risk Management

Acronyms

1. Define the following new acronyms

   No new acronyms are defined in this topic

Complete the following

2. What does the term requirements mean in the sense of this topic?

   a. ____

3. What are some examples of sources that requirements may be derived from?

   a. ____

   b. ____

   c. ____

   d. ____

   e. ____

   f. ____

   g. ____

   h. ____

4. What is determined when requirements are applied to a system?

   a. ____

5. What does the term capability mean in relation to this topic?

   a. ____

6. What are some examples of when an organization may want to divide requirements into smaller categories?

   a. ____

   b. ____

7. What can requirements pertain to?

   a. ____

b. ____

c. ____

8. In this topic, what does the term Statement of Work refer to?

a. ____

9. What can controls be viewed as?

a. ____

____

10. Why are controls implemented by an organization?

a. ____

11. What aspects can controls address?

a. ____

b. ____

c. ____

12. What do derived requirements and control parameters provide?

a. ____

13. Security and privacy controls respond to what?

a. ____

14. How do controls play a part in the lifecycle?

a. ____

b. ____

Notes:

____

____

____

____

____

____

____

____

____

Risk Management Roles and Responsibilities

https://youtu.be/yNa-Zxjvsvk

NIST SP 800-37, Task P-1

Acronyms

Define the following new acronyms

C-Suite:

____

Complete the following

1. What is the Title of task P-1?

a. ____

____

2. Who has Primary Responsibility for this task?

a. ____

b. ____

c. ____

3. What roles support this task?

a. ____

b. ____

c. ____

4. What are some potential inputs to this task?

a. ____

b. ____

5. What are the expected outputs for this task?

a. ____

____

6. Where are the roles and responsibilities for the RMF tasks listed?

    a. ____

7. Can roles be assigned to individuals internal and external to the organization?

    a. ____

8. Are there any limitations to who can be assigned to roles and responsibility?

    a. ____

9. What assigning the same individual to multiple roles and responsibilities what needs to be avoided?

    a. ____

10. Can roles be allocated to a group?

    a. ____

11. What are some references for this task?

    a. ____

    b. ____

    c. ____

Notes:

____

____

____

____

____

____

____

____

____

____

____

____

Risk Management Strategy

SP 800-37, P2

Acronyms

1. Define the following new acronyms

   There are no new acronyms in this task

Complete the following

2. What is the Title of task P-2?

   a. ____

3. Who has Primary Responsibility for this task?

   a. ____

4. What roles support this task?

   a. ____

   b. ____

   c. ____

   d. ____

5. What are some potential inputs to this task?

   a. ____

   b. ____

   c. ____

6. What are the expected outputs for this task?

   a. ____

   b. ____

7. Define risk tolerance?

     a.

____

8. What does the risk management strategy guide?

     a.

____

9. How can the risk management strategy be composed?

     a. ____

     b. ____

10. What does the risk management strategy make explicit?

     a. ____

     b. ____

     c. ____

     d. ____

     e. ____

     f. ____

11. What strategic level decisions are decisions or considerations for how senior leaders do what?

     a. ____

     b. ____

12. What does the organization risk management strategy include?

     a. ____

     b. ____

     c. ____

     d. ____

13. What does the risk management strategy connect?

     a. ____

____

14. As organizations define and implement the risk management strategies, policies, procedures, and processes, it is important that they include what?

      a. ____

15. What are some references for this task?

      a. ____

      b. ____

      c. ____

      d. ____

      e. ____

      f. ____

      g. ____

Notes:

____

____

____

____

____

____

____

____

____

____

____

____

____

____

____

____

Organizational Risk Assessment

https://youtu.be/yqE7z6eQGio

NIST SP 800-37, P-3

Acronyms

Define the following new acronyms

There are no new acronyms in this task

Complete the following

1. What is the Title of task P-3?

a. ____

2. Who has Primary Responsibility for this task?

a. ____

b. ____

c. ____

3. What roles support this task?

a. ____

b. ____

c. ____

4. What are some potential inputs to this task?

a. ____

b. ____

c. ____

d. ____

e. ____

f. ____

g. ____

h. ____

5. What are the expected outputs for this task?

      a. ____

6. Explain risk aggregation?

      a. ____

7. Describe the totality of risk?

      a.

____

____

8. Explain how segregation helps mitigate risk?

      a. ____

____

9. Should supply chains risk be assessed?

      a. ____

10. What references support this task?

      a. ____

      b. ____

      c. ____

      d. ____

      e. ____

Notes:

____

____

____

____

____

____

____

____

____

____

____

Organizationally Tailored Baselines

https://youtu.be/qktbXAKKkfc

NIST SP 800-37, P-4

Acronyms

Define the following new acronyms

There are no new acronyms in this task

Complete the following

1. What is the Title of task P-4?

    a. ____

2. Who has Primary Responsibility for this task?

    a. ____

    b. ____

3. What roles support this task?

    a. ____

    b. ____

    c. ____

    d. ____

4. What are some potential inputs to this task?

    a. ____

    b. ____

    c. ____

    d. ____

    e. ____

    f. ____

    g. ____

5. Define a control.

    a. ____

____

____

____

6. Define a control baseline.

    a. ____

____

____

7. How many baselines are defined in NIST SP 800-53/800-53B?

    a. ____

8. How many controls are in each baseline?

    a. ____

    b. ____

    c. ____

    d. ____

9. Specialized sets of controls to reduce risk and address what?

    a. ____

10. What can be used to guide the tailoring process?

    a. ____

11. By tailoring a baseline, what do we do to the control set?

    a. ____

12. Explain parameter values

    a. ____

13. Can these values be modified in the tailoring process, is so how?

    a. ____

14. Can external providers prepare tailored baselines for the organization?

    a. ____

15. If so, what limitations can be put on modifying these baselines?

    a. ____

16. What are some examples of groups that could benefit from organizationally tailored baselines?

    a. ____

    b. ____

    c. ____

    d. ____

    e. ____

    f. ____

    g. ____

    h. ____

Notes:

____

____

____

____

____

____

____

____

____

____

____

____

____

Common Control Identification

NIST SP 800-37, Task P-5

Acronyms

Define the following new acronyms

CCP: ____

Complete the following

1. What is the Title of task P-5?

    a. ____

2. Who has Primary Responsibility for this task?

    a. ____

    b. ____

3. What roles support this task?

    a. ____

    b. ____

    c. ____

    d. ____

    e. ____

    f. ____

4. What are some potential inputs to this task?

    a. ____

    b. ____

    c. ____

    d. ____

5. Explain inheritance.

    a. ____

    ____

    ____

6. What are some examples of control families that have controls that can be inherited?

    a. ____

    b. ____

    c. ____

    d. ____

    e. ____

7. Who is the owner of common controls or common control sets?

    a. ____

8. What do common control lists provide?

    a. ____

    ____

9. What are examples of levels that can be used to differentiate common control sets?

    a. ____

    b. ____

    c. ____

    d. ____

10. Explain or define what a hybrid control is?

    a. ____

    ____

    ____

11. True or False. A common control can only be provided by one common control provider.

    a. ____

12. What information about common controls is provided to the system owner?

    a. ____

13. What type of assessment must system owners complete when implementing common controls?

    a. ____

14. True or False. The common control provider must know all the information about the systems that are inheriting their common controls.

    a. ____

15. What do system owners do when a common control does not provide the needed level of protection?

    a. ____

16. Are common controls required to follow the RMF process, if so, who will serve as the AO?

    a. ____

    b. ____

17. Are common controls documented like a system?

    a. ____

18. What are common control providers responsible for?

    a. ____

    b. ____

    c. ____

    d. ____

    e. ____

19. What documentation does the common control provide present to the system owner?

    a. ____

    ____

20. Where would an organization go to start selecting controls that are candidates for becoming common controls?

    a. ____

Notes:

____

____

____

____

____

____

____

____

____

____

____

____

____

Impact Level Prioritization

NIST SP 800-37, Task P-6

Acronyms

Define the following new acronyms

There are no new acronyms introduced in this task

Complete the following

1. What is the Title of task P-6?

a. ____

2. Who has Primary Responsibility for this task?

a. ____

b. ____

3. What roles support this task?

a. ____

b. ____

c. ____

d. ____

e. ____

f. ____

g. ____

4. What are some potential inputs to this task?

    a. ____

    b. ____

    c. ____

    d. ____

    e. ____

5. What are some expected outputs to this task?

    a. ____

    b. ____

    c. ____

6. What task(s) in the CSF does this task align with?

    a. ____

7. What must be completed before this task can be completed?

    a. ____

8. What are systems categorized in accordance with?

    a. ____

9. What are the basic high-water mark categories?

    a. ____

    b. ____

    c. ____

10. What are some examples of additional granularity as defined by this task?

    a. ____

    b. ____

    c. ____

11. How does this additional granularity impact prioritization?

    a. ____

    ____

    ____

12. How can mission critical business systems be identified?

      a. ____

13. What level can impact-level prioritizations be carried out at?

      a. ____

14. True or False. CSF can be used to support impact-level prioritization.

      a. ____

Notes:

Organizational Monitoring Strategy

NIST SP 800-37, Task P-7

Acronyms

Define the following new acronyms

CM: ____

FOCI: ____

Complete the following

1. What is the Title of task P-7?

    a. ____

2. Who has Primary Responsibility for this task?

    a. ____

    b. ____

3. What roles support this task?

    a. ____

    b. ____

    c. ____

    d. ____

    e. ____

    f. ____

4. What are some potential inputs to this task?

    a. ____

    b. ____

    c. ____

5. What are some expected outputs to this task?

    a. ____

6. What task(s) in the CSF does this task align with?

    a. ____

    b. ____

7. What is an important aspect of risk management?

    a. ____

8. True or False. Supply chain risk concerns should be addressed in the continuous monitoring

strategy.

    a. ____

9. The implementation of a robust and comprehensive continuous monitoring program helps

an organization understand what?

    a. ____

10. Ongoing authorization is facilitated by what?

    a. ____

11. What does the organizational continuous monitoring strategy address?

    a. ____

    b. ____

    c. ____

12. What are some goals of the continuous monitoring strategy?

    a. ____

    b. ____

    c. ____

    d. ____

13. What are some roles that determine the strategy criteria?

    a. ____

    b. ____

    c. ____

    d. ____

    e. ____

    f. ____

    g. ____

14. What can risk management help inform in continuous monitoring strategy?

    a. ____

15. What can automation help facilitate?

    a. ____

    b. ____

16. Who is responsible for approving the continuous monitoring strategy?

    a. ____

    b. ____

Notes:

____

____

____

____

____

____

____

____

____

Mission or Business Focus

NIST SP 800-37, Task P-8

Acronyms

No new acronyms were introduced in this topic

Complete the following

1. What is the Title of task P-8?

    a. ____

2. Who has Primary Responsibility for this task?

    b. ____

3. What roles support this task?

    a. ____

    b. ____

    c. ____

    d. ____

    e. ____

    f. ____

4. What are some potential inputs to this task?

    a. ____

    b. ____

    c. ____

    d. ____

    e. ____

    d. ____

5. What are some expected outputs to this task?

    a. ____

    b. ____

    c. ____

6. What task(s) in the SDLC does this task align with?

    a. ____

    b. ____

7. What task(s) in the CSF does this task align with?

    a. ____

8. What do organizational missions and business functions influence?

    a. ____

    ____

9. What does the prioritization of missions and business functions drive?

    a. ____

    b. ____

    c. ____

    d. ____

10. What does the information elicited from stakeholders provide a more thorough understanding of what?

    a. ____

11. From the answer to question number 10 include (more specifically)?

    a. ____

    b. ____

    c. ____

12. What are some references for this task?

    a. ____

    b. ____

    c. ____

    d. ____

    e. ____

Notes:

System Stakeholders

https://youtu.be/-qzvOX6kSBI

NIST SP 800-37, Task P-9

Acronyms

No new acronyms were introduced in this topic

Complete the following

1. What is the Title of task P-9?

a. ____

2. Who has Primary Responsibility for this task?

a. ____

b. ____

3. What roles support this task?

a. ____

b. ____

c. ____

d. ____

e. ____

f. ____

4. What are some potential inputs to this task?

a. ____

b. ____

c. ____

d. ____

e. ____

f. ____

g. ____

____

5. What are some expected outputs to this task?

    a. ____

6. What task(s) in the SDLC does this task align with?

    a. ____

    b. ____

7. What task(s) in the CSF does this task align with?

    a. ____

    b. ____

8. Stakeholders are entities that have an interest in the system throughout its lifecycle for what?

    a. ____

    b. ____

    c. ____

    d. ____

    e. ____

    f. ____

9. Stakeholders may reside in the same organization or they may also reside where?

    a.

____

10. What does the information elicited from stakeholders provide a more thorough understanding of what?

    a. ____

11. What type of system may the stakeholders be impacted by?

    a. ____

    b. ____

    c. ____

12. What does communication with the stakeholders throughout the SDLC ensure?

    a. ____

    b. ____

    c. ____

13. What are some references for this task?

    a. ____

    b. ____

    c. ____

    d. ____

    e. ____

Notes:

Asset Identification

NIST SP 800-37, Task P-10

Acronyms

No new acronyms were introduced in this topic

Complete the following

1. What is the Title of task P-10?

a. ____

2. Who has Primary Responsibility for this task?

a. ____

3. What roles support this task?

a. ____

b. ____

c. ____

d. ____

e. ____

f. ____

4. What are some potential inputs to this task?

a. ____

b. ____

c. ____

d. ____

e. ____

f. ____

g. ____

h. ____

5. What are some expected outputs to this task?

a. ____

6. What task(s) in the SDLC does this task align with?

a. ____

b. ____

7. What task(s) in the CSF does this task align with?

a. ____

8. What are the two main types of assets?

a. ____

b. ____

9. What are some examples of assets that are in the same class as Human Elements?

a. ____

b. ____

10. What are some examples of assets that are not physical in nature?

a. ____

b. ____

c. ____

d. ____

e. ____

11. What type of asset can an information asset be (from the types defined in #8)?

    a. ____

    b. ____

12. What are some other types of assets that fit the category of #11?

    a. ____

    b. ____

13. What context of the use of assets that stakeholders could be concerned about?

    a. ____

    b. ____

    c. ____

14. Where is one location that assets can be documented?

    a. ____

15. What are some references for this task?

    a. ____

    b. ____

    c. ____

    d. ____

    e. ____

Notes:

____

____

____

____

____

____

____

____

____

____

____

____

Authorization Boundary

NIST SP 800-37, Task P11

Acronyms

No new acronyms were introduced in this topic

Complete the following

1. What is the Title of task P-11?

a. ____

2. Who has Primary Responsibility for this task?

a. ____

3. What roles support this task?

a. ____

b. ____

c. ____

d. ____

e. ____

f. ____

4. What are some potential inputs to this task?

a. ____

b. ____

c. ____

d. ____

e. ____

f. ____

5. What are some expected outputs to this task?

    a. ____

6. What task(s) in the SDLC does this task align with?

    a. ____

    b. ____

7. Authorization Boundaries Establish The Scope Of Protection For Information Systems, what does this mean?

    a. ____

8. Who determines authorization boundaries?

    a. ____

9. Why is clear delineation of boundaries important?

    a. ____

    b. ____

10. What the purpose of a system element?

    a. ____

    b. ____

11. What are some things included in system elements?

    a. ____

    b. ____

    c. ____

12. What is defined by the term system?

    a. ____

13. How many authorization boundaries does a system have?

    a. ____

14. Who should be included in collaboration for systems that process PII?

    a. ____

15. Understanding the authorization boundary and what will occur beyond it may influence what?

    a. ____

16. May Be Used To Delineate What Constitutes Authorization Boundaries with external providers?

    a. ____

17. What are some references for this task?

    a. ____

    b. ____

    c. ____

    d. ____

    e. ____

    f. ____

Notes:

Information Types

NIST SP 800-37, Task P-12

Acronyms

NARA-CUI: ____

Complete the following

1. What is the Title of task P-12?

    a. ____

2. Who has Primary Responsibility for this task?

    a. ____

    b. ____

3. What roles support this task?

    a. ____

    b. ____

    c. ____

4. What are some potential inputs to this task?

    a. ____

    b. ____

    c. ____

    d. ____

5. What are some expected outputs to this task?

    a. ____

6. What task(s) in the SDLC does this task align with?

    a. ____

    b. ____

7. Identifying the types of information, a system processes is important in determining what?

     a. ____

8. What type of information does NARA define?

     a. ____

9. What NIST document will help a system owner in determining information types?

     a. ____

10. Information types are confirmed by who?

     a. ____

     b. ____

11. What are some references for this task?

     a. ____

     b. ____

     c. ____

     d. ____

     e. ____

     f. ____

Notes:____

____

____

____

____

____

____

____

____

____

____

Information Life Cycle

NIST SP 800-37, Task P-13

Acronyms

No new acronyms were introduced in this topic

Complete the following

1. What is the Title of task P-13?

a. ____

2. Who has Primary Responsibility for this task?

a. ____

b. ____

c. ____

3. What roles support this task?

a. ____

b. ____

c. ____

d. ____

e. ____

f. ____

g. ____

4. What are some potential inputs to this task?

    a. ____

    b. ____

    c. ____

    d. ____

    e. ____

    f. ____

    g. ____

5. What are some expected outputs to this task?

    a. ____

    b. ____

6. What task(s) in the SDLC does this task align with?

    a. ____

    b. ____

7. What tasks in the CSF does this task align with?

    a. ____

    b. ____

8. What are the phases in the information life cycle?

    a. ____

    b. ____

    c. ____

    d. ____

    e. ____

    f. ____

9. Identification and understanding of the information life cycle helps insure what?

    a. ____

    b. ____

    c. ____

    d. ____

10. What does a data map provide?

    a. ____

____

11. Why is it important for organizations to consider the appropriate delineation of the authorization boundary?

    a. ____

12. Why is Identifying And Understanding The Information Life Cycle Is Particularly Relevant for the assessment of security and privacy risk?

    a. ____

13. What are some references for this task?

    a. ____

    b. ____

    c. ____

    d. ____

    e. ____

Notes:____

____

____

____

____

____

____

____

____

____

____

____

____

Risk Assessment - System

https://youtu.be/7X4OObUX66M

NIST SP 800-37, Task P-14

Acronyms

No new acronyms were introduced in this topic

Complete the following

1. What is the Title of task P-14?

    a. ____

2. Who has Primary Responsibility for this task?

    a. ____

    b. ____

    c. ____

3. What roles support this task?

    a. ____

    b. ____

    c. ____

    d. ____

    e. ____

4. What are some potential inputs to this task?

    a. ____

    b. ____

    c. ____

    d. ____

    e. ____

    f. ____

    g. ____

    h. ____

    i. ____

    j. ____

    k. ____

5. What are some expected outputs to this task?

    a. ____

6. What task(s) in the SDLC does this task align with?

    a. ____

    b. ____

7. What tasks in the CSF does this task align with?

    a. ____

    b. ____

8. Why do organizations conduct security and privacy risk assessments?

    a. ____

9. Assessment of security risk includes what?

    a. ____

    b. ____

    c. ____

    d. ____

10. Assets are prioritized based on what?

    a. ____

____

11. How is loss defined?

    a. ____

____

12. Loss Consequences May Be?

    a. ____

    b. ____

13. Interpretations of information loss may include what?

    a. ____

    b. ____

    c. ____

14. Loss of a function or service may be interpreted as what?

    a. ____

    b. ____

    c. ____

    d. ____

    e. ____

15. Physical consequences of compromise can include what?

    a. ____

    b. ____

    c. ____

    d. ____

    e. ____

16. Prioritization of assets is based on what?

    a. ____

    b. ____

    c. ____

    d. ____

    e. ____

    f. ____

17. Asset priority translates to what?

    a. ____

    b. ____

    c. ____

18. Privacy risk assessments are conducted to determine what?

    a. ____

19. Contextual Factors Can Include (but are not limited to) what?

    a. ____

    b. ____

    c. ____

    d. ____

20. Privacy risks to individuals may create what?

    a. ____

    b. ____

    c. ____

21. Risk assessments are also conducted on an external provider for what phases of a system life?

    a. ____

    b. ____

    c. ____

    d. ____

    e. ____

    f. ____

22. The impact of a risk may be what?

    a. ____

    b. ____

    c. ____

    d. ____

23. Supply chain risk assessments consider what vulnerabilities?

    a. ____

24. Supply chain risk assessments can include information from what?

    a. ____

    b. ____

    c. ____

25. Risk assessment results are used to do what?

    a. ____

    b. ____

    c. ____

    d. ____

    e. ____

26. What are some references for this topic?

    a. ____

    b. ____

    c. ____

    d. ____

    e. ____

    f. ____

    g. ____

    h. ____

    i. ____

    j. ____

    k. ____

    l. ____

    m. ____

    n. ____

Notes:

____

____

____

____

____

____

____

____

____

____

Requirements Definition

NIST SP 800-37, Task P-15

Acronyms

No new acronyms were introduced in this topic

Complete the following

1. What is the Title of task P-15?

    a. ____

2. Who has Primary Responsibility for this task?

    a. ____

    b. ____

    c. ____

    d. ____

3. What roles support this task?

    a. ____

    b. ____

    c. ____

    d. ____

    e. ____

    f. ____

    g. ____

    h. ____

4. What are some potential inputs to this task?

a. ____

b. ____

c. ____

d. ____

e. ____

f. ____

g. ____

h. ____

i. ____

j. ____

k. ____

l. ____

5. What are some expected outputs to this task?

a. ____

6. What task(s) in the SDLC does this task align with?

a. ____

b. ____

7. What tasks in the CSF does this task align with?

a. ____

b. ____

8. Protection needs are an expression of what?

a. ____

9. Protection Needs Include what?

a. ____

b. ____

10. The protection needs reflect what?

    a. ____

    b. ____

    c. ____

    d. ____

    e. ____

11. What are some sources of security and privacy requirements?

    a. ____

    b. ____

    c. ____

    d. ____

    e. ____

    f. ____

    g. ____

    h. ____

12. What do security and privacy requirements guide and inform?

    a. ____

    b. ____

13. What are some references for this topic?

    a. ____

    b. ____

    c. ____

    d. ____

    e. ____

    f. ____

Notes:

____

____

____

____

____

Enterprise Architecture

https://youtu.be/K7rMFE16yhI

NIST SP 800-37, Task P-16

Acronyms

No new acronyms were introduced in this topic

Complete the following

1. What is the Title of task P-16?

  a. ____

2. Who has Primary Responsibility for this task?

  a. ____

  b. ____

  c. ____

  d. ____

3. What roles support this task?

  a. ____

  b. ____

  c. ____

  d. ____

  e. ____

  f. ____

4. What are some potential inputs to this task?

  a. ____

  b. ____

  c. ____

  d. ____

  e. ____

  f. ____

5. What are some expected outputs to this task?

    a. ____

    b. ____

    c. ____

    d. ____

6. What task(s) in the SDLC does this task align with?

    a. ____

    b. ____

7. What tasks in the CSF does this task align with?

    a. ____

8. What does Enterprise Architecture maximize?

    a. ____

    b. ____

9. Enterprise architecture can provide greater understanding of what?

    a. ____

    b. ____

10. Enterprise architecture also provides an opportunity for what?

    a. ____

    b. ____

11. Why is the placement of a system within the enterprise architecture important?

    a. ____

    b. ____

12. What other types of architecture are Integral Parts Of The Enterprise Architecture?

    a. ____

    b. ____

13. The security and privacy architectures provide what?

    a. ____

    b. ____

14. What are some references for this topic?

    a. ____

    b. ____

    c. ____

    d. ____

    e. ____

    f. ____

Notes:

____

____

____

____

____

____

____

____

____

____

____

____

Requirements Allocation

https://youtu.be/o7jcRZWcVd0

NIST SP 800-37, Task P-17

Acronyms

No new acronyms were introduced in this topic

Complete the following

1. What is the Title of task P-17?

    a. ____

2. Who has Primary Responsibility for this task?

    a. ____

    b. ____

    c. ____

    d. ____

3. What roles support this task?

    a. ____

    b. ____

    c. ____

    d. ____

    e. ____

    f. ____

4. What are some potential inputs to this task?

    a. ____

    b. ____

    c. ____

    d. ____

    e. ____

    f. ____

    g. ____

    h. ____

5. What are some expected outputs to this task?

    a. ____

6. What task(s) in the SDLC does this task align with?

    a. ____

    b. ____

7. What tasks in the CSF does this task align with?

    a. ____

8. Why are security and privacy requirements allocated?

    a. ____

    b. ____

9. What determines where controls will be implemented?

    a. ____

    b. ____

10. What are some references for this topic?

    a. ____

    b. ____

    c. ____

    d. ____

    e. ____

Notes:____

____

____

____

____

____

____

System Registration

NIST SP 800-37, Task P-18

Acronyms

No new acronyms were introduced in this topic

Complete the following

1. What is the Title of task P-18?

    a. ____

2. Who has Primary Responsibility for this task?

    a. ____

3. What roles support this task?

    a. ____

    b. ____

    c. ____

    d. ____

4. What are some potential inputs to this task?

    a. ____

    b. ____

5. What are some expected outputs to this task?

    a. ____

6. What task(s) in the SDLC does this task align with?

    a. ____

    b. ____

7. What tasks in the CSF does this task align with?

    a. ____

8. System registration informs the governing organization of what?

    a. ____

    b. ____

    c. ____

9. System registration provides organizations with what?

    a. ____

    b. ____

    c. ____

10. When is system categorization added to the system registration?

    a. ____

11. What are some references for this topic?

    a. ____

Notes:

____

____

____

____

____

____

____

____

____

____

____

____

____

____

System Description

https://youtu.be/Oo-zL5pdxUY

NIST SP 800-37, Task C-1

Acronyms

No new acronyms were introduced in this topic

Complete the following

1. What is the Title of task C-1?

    a. ____

2. Who has Primary Responsibility for this task?

    a. ____

3. What roles support this task?

    a. ____

    b. ____

    c. ____

    d. ____

    e. ____

4. What are some potential inputs to this task?

    a. ____

    b. ____

    c. ____

    d. ____

    e. ____

    f. ____

    g. ____

    h. ____

    i. ____

    j. ____

5. What are some expected outputs to this task?

    a. ____

6. What task(s) in the SDLC does this task align with?

    a. ____

    b. ____

7. What tasks in the CSF does this task align with?

    a. ____

8. The description of the system characteristics is documented of included in what?

    a. ____

    b. ____

    c. ____

9. How is level of detail determined?

    a. ____

    ____

    ____

10. True or False. Once the system description is documented it cannot be updated.

    a. ____

11. What are some references for this topic?

    a. ____

    b. ____

Notes:____

____

____

____

____

____

____

____

Security Categorization

NIST SP 800-37, Task C-2

Acronyms

No new acronyms were introduced in this topic

Complete the following

1. What is the Title of task C-2?

a. ____

2. Who has Primary Responsibility for this task?

a. ____

b. ____

c. ____

3. What roles support this task?

a. ____

b. ____

c. ____

d. ____

e. ____

f. ____

g. ____

h. ____

i. ____

4. What are some potential inputs to this task?

    a. ____

    b. ____

    c. ____

    d. ____

    e. ____

    f. ____

    g. ____

    h. ____

    i. ____

5. What are some expected outputs to this task?

    a. ____

    b. ____

6. What task(s) in the SDLC does this task align with?

    a. ____

    b. ____

7. What tasks in the CSF does this task align with?

    a. ____

    b. ____

    c. ____

    d. ____

    e. ____

8. Security Categorization Determinations Consider what?

    a. ____

    ____

    ____

9. Organizations Have Flexibility In Conducting A Security Categorization Using what?

    a. ____

    b. ____

    c. ____

10. Cooperation and collaboration helps to ensure what?

    a. ____

    ____

11. Who considers the results from the security risk assessment as a part of the security categorization decision?

    a. ____

    b. ____

12. Where is the security categorization information documented?

    a. ____

    b. ____

13. Why would the security categorization results for the system be further refined?

    a. ____

    ____

14. What are some references for this task?

    a. ____

    b. ____

    c. ____

    d. ____

    e. ____

    f. ____

    g. ____

    h. ____

    i. ____

    j. ____

    k. ____

Notes:

____

____

____

____

____

Security Categorization Review and Approval

NIST SP 800-37, Task C-3

Acronyms

No new acronyms were introduced in this topic

Complete the following

1. What is the Title of task C-3?

    a. ____

2. Who has Primary Responsibility for this task?

    a. ____

    b. ____

    c. ____

3. What roles support this task?

    a. ____

    b. ____

    c. ____

    d. ____

4. What are some potential inputs to this task?

    a. ____

    b. ____

    c. ____

5. What are some expected outputs to this task?

    a. ____

6. What task(s) in the SDLC does this task align with?

    a. ____

    b. ____

7. What tasks in the CSF does this task align with?

    a. ____

8. Who approves the plan before the AO for information systems that process PII?

    a. ____

9. What does the AO review the category selected for the information system to ensure?

    a. ____

    b. ____

10. Who does The Authorizing Official Collaborates With?

    a. ____

    b. ____

11. Why do they collaborate with those roles?

    a. ____

    b. ____

12. What specific guidance can the AO provide to the system owner?

    a. ____

    ____

13. What happens if the categorization is not approved?

    a. ____

    b. ____

14. What are some references for this task?

    a. ____

    b. ____

    c. ____

    d. ____

    e. ____

    f. ____

Notes:____

____

____

____

Control Selection

NIST SP 800-37, Task S-1

Acronyms

Define the following new acronyms

No new acronyms are defined in this task

Complete the following

1. What is the title of task S-1?

a. ____

2. What are some potential inputs for this task?

a. ____

b. ____

c. ____

d. ____

e. ____

f. ____

g. ____

h. ____

i. ____

j. ____

k. ____

3. What is the expected output from this task?

a. ____

4. Who has primary responsibility for this task?

a. ____

b. ____

5. What roles support this task?

    a. ____

    b. ____

    c. ____

    d. ____

    e. ____

    f. ____

6. How does this task align with the SDLC?

    a. ____

    b. ____

7. How does this task align with the CSF?

    a. ____

8. What are two approaches for the initial selection of controls?

    a. ____

    b. ____

9. According to this task what are control baselines?

    a. ____

    ____

10. What is the control baseline the starting point for?

    a. ____

11. What document provides information for Federal baselines?

    a. ____

12. What does the privacy program use baselines for?

    a. ____

    ____

13. In what task does control baseline tailoring occur?

    a. ____

14. What is the difference between organization-generated control selection and the baseline approach?

    a. ____

15. What is one reason an organization would use organization-generated controls over the baseline approach?

    a. ____

    ____

16. What is developed using either the baseline control selection approach or the organization-generated control selection approach?

    a. ____

17. The generated requirements from this task can be used for what?

    a. ____

    ____

18. What can the NIST CSF be used to develop?

    a. ____

19. Must the organization select and use only one approach?

    a. ____

20. What are some references for this task?

    a. ____

    b. ____

    c. ____

    d. ____

    e. ____

    f. ____

    g. ____

    h. ____

    i. ____

    j. ____

    k. ____

Notes:

____

____

____

Control Tailoring

https://youtu.be/_2wCQdJy2Q0
NIST SP 800-37, Task S-2

Acronyms

Define the following new acronyms

No new acronyms are defined in this task

Complete the following

1. What is the title of this task?

   a. ____

2. What are some potential inputs for this task?

   a. ____

   b. ____

   c. ____

   d. ____

   e. ____

   e. ____

   f. ____

   g. ____

   h. ____

3. What is the expected output from this task?

   a. ____

4. Who has primary responsibility for this task?

   a. ____

   b. ____

5. What roles support this task?

    a. ____

    b. ____

    c. ____

    d. ____

    e. ____

    f. ____

    g. ____

6. How does this task align with the SDLC?

    a. ____

    b. ____

7. How does this task align with the CSF?

    a. ____

8. What are some examples of factors used for tailoring baselines?

    a. ____

    b. ____

    c. ____

    d. ____

    e. ____

9. What does the tailoring process include?

    a. ____

    b. ____

    c. ____

    d. ____

    e. ____

10. Who determines the amount of detail to include in tailoring justifications?

    a. ____

11. What should tailoring determinations be consistent with?

    a. ____

    b. ____

12. What does the tailoring process include?

    a. ____

    b. ____

    c. ____

    d. ____

13. System specific controls satisfy security and privacy requirements allocated to what?

    a. ____

14. What do organizations use the risk assessment to guide?

    a. ____

15. What does the privacy risk assessment influence?

    a. ____

16. How does the risk assessment impact common control selection?

    a. ____

       ____

    b. ____

       ____

17. What else can an organization consider when tailoring a control baseline?

    a. ____

    b. ____

    c. ____

18. What are some references for this task?

    a. ____

    b. ____

    c. ____

    d. ____

    e. ____

    f. ____

    g. ____

Notes:

____

____

____

____

____

____

Bonus: Video Illustrating Control Tailoring

https://youtu.be/3nUH7B4OIVQ

Notes:

____

____

____

____

____

____

Control Allocation

NIST SP 800-37, Task S-3

Acronyms

Define the following new acronyms

No new acronyms are defined in this task

Complete the following

1. What is the title of this task?

a. ____

2. What are some potential inputs for this task?

a. ____

b. ____

c. ____

d. ____

e. ____

f. ____

g. ____

h. ____

i. ____

j. ____

k. ____

l. ____

3. What is the expected output from this task?

a. ____

4. Who has primary responsibility for this task?

    a. ____

    b. ____

    c. ____

    d. ____

5. What roles support this task?

    a. ____

    b. ____

    c. ____

    d. ____

    e. ____

    f. ____

    g. ____

6. How does this task align with the SDLC?

    a. ____

    b. ____

7. How does this task align with the CSF?

    a. ____

    b. ____

8. What are the three types of control designations an organization will use in designating controls?

    a. ____

    b. ____

    c. ____

9. Controls providing a specific security or privacy capability are only allocated to what?

    a. ____

10. The security categorization, privacy risk assessment, security and privacy architectures, and the allocation of controls work together to do what?

    a. ____

11. Security and privacy requirements allocated to the system, system elements, and the environment of operation guide and inform what?

    a. ____

12. Common controls that are made available by the organization during what step of the RMF?

    a. ____

13. Hybrid controls satisfy security and privacy requirements allocated to what and why?

    a. ____

    ____

14. system-specific controls satisfy security and privacy requirements allocated to what?

    a. ____

    ____

15. What are some references for this task?

    a. ____

    b. ____

    c. ____

    d. ____

    e. ____

Notes:

____

____

____

____

____

____

____

____

____

____

____

Documentation of Planned Control Implementation

NIST SP 800-37, TaskS-4

Acronyms

Define the following new acronyms

No new acronyms are defined in this task

Complete the following

1. What is the title of this task?

    a. ____

2. What are some potential inputs for this task?

    a. ____

    b. ____

    c. ____

    d. ____

    e. ____

    f. ____

    g. ____

    h. ____

    i. ____

3. What is the expected output from this task?

    a. ____

4. Who has primary responsibility for this task?

    a. ____

    b. ____

5. What roles support this task?

    a. ____

    b. ____

    c. ____

    d. ____

    e. ____

    f. ____

    g. ____

6. How does this task align with the SDLC?

    a. ____

    b. ____

7. How does this task align with the CSF?

    a. ____

8. Security and privacy plans contain an overview of what?

    a. ____

    b. ____

    c. ____

9. The plans describe the intended application of what?

    a. ____

      ____

      ____

10. The control documentation describes what?

    a. ____

      ____

11. What does the description include?

    a. ____

    b. ____

    c. ____

12. For hybrid controls, the organization specifies in the system-level plans the parts of what?

    a. ____

      ____

13. In what two ways can the organization develop plans?

    a. ____

      ____

15. Who must collaborate if using a consolidated plan?

    a. ____

    b. ____

16. If using separate system security plans and privacy plans, organizations must do what?

    a. ____

17. Who reviews and approved the privacy plan before it is provided to the AO?

    a. ____

18. Documentation of the planned control implementation allows for what?

    a. ____

19. Documentation for control implementations follows what?

    a. ____

20. What program supports documentation of privacy risk considerations and the implementations intended to mitigate them?

    a. ____

21. For controls that are mechanism-based, organizations take advantage of what?

    a. ____

22. What are some references for this task?

    a. ____

    b. ____

    c. ____

    d. ____

    e. ____

    f. ____

    g. ____

    h. ____

    i. ____

    j. ____

    k. ____

Notes:

Continuous Monitoring Strategy - System

NIST SP 800-37, TaskS-5

Acronyms

Define the following new acronyms

No new acronyms are defined in this task

Complete the following

1. What is the title of this task?

    a. ____

2. What are some potential inputs for this task?

    a. ____

    b. ____

    c. ____

    d. ____

    e. ____

3. What is the expected output from this task?

    a. ____

4. Who has primary responsibility for this task?

    a. ____

    b. ____

5. What roles support this task?

    a. ____

    b. ____

    c. ____

    d. ____

    e. ____

    f. ____

g. ____

h. ____

i. ____

j. ____

k. ____

l. ____

m. ____

n. ____

6. How does this task align with the SDLC?

a. ____

b. ____

7. How does this task align with the CSF?

a. ____

b. ____

8. What is an important aspect of risk management?

a. ____

9. An effective continuous monitoring strategy at the system level is developed and implemented in coordination with what?

a. ____

10. The system-level continuous monitoring strategy is consistent with an supplements what?

a. ____

11. The system-level strategy addresses monitoring of what?

a. ____

____

12. The system level continuous monitoring strategy, consistent with the organizational monitoring strategy, defines what?

a. ____

b. ____

c. ____

13. The system-level strategy identifies the frequency of monitoring of what?

    a. ____

    ____

14. The frequency criteria at the system level reflect what?

    a. ____

    ____

15. What may cause controls to require more frequent assessment?

    a. ____

    b. ____

    c. ____

16. The approach to control assessments during continuous monitoring may include what?

    a. ____

    b. ____

    c. ____

17. When does the monitoring of controls begin?

    a. ____

16. When does the monitoring of controls end?

    a. ____

17. What are some references for this task?

    a. ____

    b. ____

    c. ____

    d. ____

    e. ____

    f. ____

    g. ____

    h. ____

    i. ____

    j. ____

    k. ____

Notes:

Plan Review and Approval

NIST SP 800-37, Task S-6

Acronyms

Define the following new acronyms

No new acronyms are defined in this task

Complete the following

1. What is the title of this task?

    a. ____

2. What are some potential inputs for this task?

    a. ____

    b. ____

3. What is the expected output from this task?

    a. ____

4. Who has primary responsibility for this task?

    a. ____

    b. ____

5. What roles support this task?

    a. ____

    b. ____

    c. ____

    d. ____

    e. ____

    f. ____

6. How does this task align with the SDLC?

    a. ____

    b. ____

7. How does this task align with the CSF?

    a. ____

8. The security and privacy plan review by the authorizing official or designated representative with support from who?

    a. ____

    b. ____

    c. ____

    d. ____

9. What does the AO determine?

    a. ____

    b. ____

    c. ____

10. What occurs is the plan is determined to be unacceptable to the AO?

    a. ____

11. What occurs if the plans are determined to be acceptable to the AO?

    a. ____

12. When the AO (or AODR) approved the plan what are they agreeing to?

    a. ____

    b. ____

    ____

    ____

13. When is the level of effort established?

    a. ____

14. What are some references for this task?

    a. ____

    b. ____

    c. ____

    d. ____

    e. ____

    f. ____

Notes:

____

____

____

____

____

____

____

____

____

____

____

____

____

____

____

____

Control Implementation

NIST SP 800-37, Task I-1

Acronyms

Define the following new acronyms

No new acronyms are defined in this task

Complete the following

1. What is the title of this task?

a. ____

2. What are some potential inputs for this task?

a. ____

b. ____

c. ____

d. ____

e. ____

f. ____

g. ____

h. ____

i. ____

j. ____

k. ____

3. What is the expected output from this task?

a. ____

4. Who has primary responsibility for this task?

a. ____

b. ____

5. What roles support this task?

    a. ____

    b. ____

    c. ____

    d. ____

    e. ____

    f. ____

    g. ____

    h. ____

    i. ____

6. How does this task align with the SDLC?

    a. ____

    b. ____

7. How does this task align with the CSF?

    a. ____

    b. ____

8. What document describes how the controls are to be implemented?

    a. ____

9. The control implementation is consistent with what two architectures?

    a. ____

    b. ____

10. When do organizations use best practices?

    a. ____

    ____

11. Risk assessments guides and informs what?

    a. ____

    ____

12. Mandatory configuration settings are implemented in accordance with what?

    a. ____

    ____

13. What is an example of a system that the organization would have no direct control over?

    a. ____

14. When considering systems that the organization has no direct control over, what can the organization consider when looking to validate the systems?

    a. ____

    ____

    ____

15. The tests, evaluations, and validations consider products in what?

    a. ____

    b. ____

16. Assurance requirements are directed at what?

    a. ____

    b. ____

    c. ____

17. System owners can refer to what regarding the adequacy of the controls inherited by their systems?

    a. ____

18. What must the system owner do when a common control does not meet the requirements for the system inheriting the control?

    a. ____

    ____

19. What can the system owner do if there are gaps in the security or privacy requirements between the system and common controls?

    a. ____

    ____

20. Conducting assessments in parallel with the development and implementation phases of the SDLC facilitates early identification of what?

    a. ____

21. When Issues are discovered during these assessments who can be turned to for resolution?

      a. ____

22. The results of the initial control assessments can also be used for what?

      a. ____

23. What are some references for this task?

      a. ____

      b. ____

      c. ____

      d. ____

      e. ____

      f. ____

      g. ____

      h. ____

Notes:

____

____

____

____

____

____

____

____

____

____

____

Update Control Implementation Information

NIST SP 800-37, Task I-2

Acronyms

Define the following new acronyms

No new acronyms are defined in this task

Complete the following

1. What is the title of this task?

    a. ____

2. What are some potential inputs for this task?

    a. ____

    b. ____

3. What is the expected output from this task?

    a. ____

    b. ____

4. Who has primary responsibility for this task?

    a. ____

    b. ____

5. What roles support this task?

    a. ____

    b. ____

    c. ____

    d. ____

    e. ____

f. ____

g. ____

h. ____

i. ____

6. How does this task align with the SDLC?

a. ____

b. ____

7. How does this task align with the CSF?

a. ____

b. ____

8. Despite the control implementation details in the security and privacy plans and the system design documents, what may happen?

a. ____

9. The updates include revised descriptions of implemented controls include what?

a. ____

b. ____

c. ____

10. Why is documenting the "as implemented" control information is essential?

a. ____

b. ____

c. ____

d. ____

11. What are some references for this task?

a. ____

b. ____

c. ____

Notes:

____

____

____

____

Assessor Selection

NIST SP 800-37, Task A-1

Acronyms

Define the following new acronyms

No new acronyms are defined in this task

Complete the following

1. What is the title of this task?

    a. ____

2. What are some potential inputs for this task?

    a. ____

    b. ____

    c. ____

    d. ____

    e. ____

    f. ____

    g. ____

    h. ____

3. What is the expected output from this task?

    a. ____

4. Who has primary responsibility for this task?

    a. ____

    b. ____

5. What roles support this task?

    a. ____

    b. ____

    c. ____

6. How does this task align with the SDLC?

    a. ____

    b. ____

    c. ____

7. How does this task align with the CSF?

    a. ____

8. What does the organization consider when selecting control assessors?

    a. ____

    b. ____

9. The control assessor should also have general knowledge of what?

    a. ____

    ____

10. In organizations where the assessment capability is centrally managed, who may have the responsibility of selecting and managing the control assessors?

    a. ____

11. What is an independent assessor?

    a. ____

12. What does impartiality mean?

    a. ____

    ____

13. Who can the AO consult with to determine the independence of the assessor?

    a. ____

    b. ____

    c. ____

    d. ____

14. The system privacy officer is responsible for what?

     a. ____

     b. ____

     c. ____

15. Who is responsible for conducting assessments of privacy controls and documenting the results of the assessments?

     a. ____

16. Early identification and selection of assessors allows organizations to do what?

     a. ____

       ____

17. The senior agency official for privacy is responsible for providing privacy information to who?

     a. ____

18. What are some references to this task?

     a. ____

     b. ____

     c. ____

     d. ____

Notes:

____

____

____

____

____

____

____

____

____

____

____

Assessment Plan

NIST SP 800-37, Task A-2

Acronyms

Define the following new acronyms

No new acronyms are defined in this task

Complete the following

1. What is the title of this task?

    a. ____

2. What are some potential inputs for this task?

    a. ____

    b. ____

    c. ____

    d. ____

    e. ____

    f. ____

    g. ____

    h. ____

    i. ____

3. What is the expected output from this task?

    a. ____

4. Who has primary responsibility for this task?

    a. ____

    b. ____

    c. ____

5. What roles support this task?

    a. ____

    b. ____

    c. ____

    d. ____

    e. ____

    f. ____

    g. ____

6. How does this task align with the SDLC?

    a. ____

    b. ____

    c. ____

7. How does this task align with the CSF?

    a. ____

8. The control assessment plan is developed based on information provided in what documents?

    a. ____

    b. ____

    c. ____

9. When the organization develops an integrated assessment plan, what types of controls are assessed?

    a. ____

    b. ____

10. Assessment plans also provide the objectives for what?

    a. ____

11. Assessment plans also provide the procedures for what?

    a. ____

12. Assessment plans reflect the type of assessment the organization is conducting, including what examples?

    a. ____

    b. ____

    c. ____

    d. ____

    e. ____

    f. ____

    g. ____

13. Who reviews and approves the assessment plan?

    a. ____

    b. ____

14. What is the plan reviewed to ensure consistency with?

    a. ____

    b. ____

    c. ____

15. Approved assessment plans establish expectations for what?

    a. ____

    b. ____

16. The organization can request security and privacy assessment plans and assessments results or evidence from the external provider through what?

    a. ____

    b. ____

    c. ____

    d. ____

    e. ____

17. What are some references for this task?

    a. _______________________________________

    b. _______________________________________

    c. _______________________________________

    d. _______________________________________

    e. _______________________________________

Notes:

Control Assessment

NIST SP 800-37, Task A-3

Acronyms

Define the following new acronyms

No new acronyms are defined in this task

Complete the following

1. What is the title of this task?

   a. ____

2. What are some potential inputs for this task?

   a. ____

   b. ____

   c. ____

3. What is the expected output from this task?

   a. ____

4. Who has primary responsibility for this task?

   a. ____

5. What roles support this task?

    a. ____

    b. ____

    c. ____

    d. ____

    e. ____

    f. ____

    g. ____

    h. ____

    i. ____

6. How does this task align with the SDLC?

    a. ____

    b. ____

    c. ____

7. How does this task align with the CSF?

    a. ____

8. Control assessments determine what?

    a. ____

    b. ____

    c. ____

    ____

9. The System Owner, Common Control Provider, And/or Organization Rely On the assessors what?

    a. ____

    b. ____

10. Who serves as the control assessor for the privacy controls?

    a. ____

11. What do Controls Implemented To Achieve Both Security And Privacy Objectives Require?

    a. ____

12. What are The Assessor Findings considered, and what do they determine?

    a. ____

    b. ____

13. Control Assessments Occur As Early As Practicable In The SDLC are referred to as what?

    a. ____

14. What do the assessments in question 14 validate?

    a. ____

    b. ____

15. What are some examples of developmental testing and evaluation activities?

    a. ____

    b. ____

    c. ____

16. Assessments made prior to source selection during the procurement process are put in place to assess what?

    a. ____

17. The results of control assessments conducted during the SDLC are reused to avoid what?

    a. ____

    b. ____

18. What does the use of automation help in conducting control assessments?

    a. ____

    b. ____

19. When iterative development processes (e.g., agile development) are employed, what is the impact on the assessment?

    a. ____

20. Are common controls assessed as part of the system level assessment?

    a. ____

21. Organizations ensure that assessors have access to what types of information to ensure successful assessments?

     a. ____

     b. ____

     c. ____

     d. ____

     e. ____

     f. ____

22. Who determines assessor independence?

     a. ____

23. Organizations may choose to make the risk management process more efficient and cost-effective by doing what?

     a. ____

24. Assessment results supporting an authorization to use are examples of what principle?

     a. ____

25. What are some references for this task?

     a. ____

     b. ____

     c. ____

Notes:

____

____

____

____

____

____

____

____

____

____

____

Assessment Reports

Acronyms

Define the following new acronyms

No new acronyms are defined in this task

Complete the following

1. What is the title of this task?

    a. ____

2. What are some potential inputs for this task?

    a. ____

3. What is the expected output from this task?

    a. ____

    ____

4. Who has primary responsibility for this task?

    a. ____

5. What roles support this task?

    a. ____

    b. ____

    c. ____

    d. ____

6. How does this task align with the SDLC?

    a. ____

    b. ____

    c. ____

7. How does this task align with the CSF?

    a. ____

8. What is documented in the assessment reports?

    a. ____

9. The assessment reports include information based on assessor findings necessary to determine what?

    a. ____

    ____

10. Assessment reports are an important factor in a determining what?

    a. ____

    ____

11. Are organizations required to only use one report format?

    a. ____

12. Control assessment results obtained during the system development lifecycle are documented in what type of document?

    a. ____

13. The executive summary provides authorizing officials and other interested individuals in the organization with an abbreviated version of what?

    a. ____

    ____

14. What are some references for this task?

    a. ____

    b. ____

Notes:

____

____

____

____

____

____

Remediation Actions

NIST SP 800-37, TaskA-5

Acronyms

Define the following new acronyms

No new acronyms are defined in this task

Complete the following

1. What is the title of this task?

    a. ____

2. What are some potential inputs for this task?

    a. ____

    b. ____

    c. ____

    d. ____

3. What is the expected output from this task?

    a. ____

    b. ____

    c. ____

    d. ____

4. Who has primary responsibility for this task?

    a. ____

    b. ____

    c. ____

5. What roles support this task?

    a. ____

    b. ____

    c. ____

    d. ____

    e. ____

    f. ____

    g. ____

    h. ____

    i. ____

    j. ____

    k. ____

6. How does this task align with the SDLC?

    a. ____

    b. ____

    c. ____

7. How does this task align with the CSF?

    a. ____

8. The security and privacy assessment reports describe what?

    a. ____

    b. ____

9. If the AO decides that certain findings represent significant, unacceptable risk, what is required?

    a. ____

10. What should be done if an assessment finding can be quickly and easily remediated with existing resources?

    a. ____

11. The control reassessments determine what?

    a. ____

    ____

    ____

12. What do the assessors update with the findings from the reassessment?

    a. ____

13. When the control assessor updates the document in 13, do they change the original results?

    a. ____

14. At the completion of the control assessments what document(s) should be updated to reflect the accurate description of the implemented controls?

    a. ____

    b. ____

15. What does an addendum to the security and privacy assessment reports that provide?

    a. ____

    ____

16. Does the addendum does change or influence the initial assessor findings provided in the reports?

    a. ____

    ____

17. The issue resolution process can also ensure that only substantive items are identified and transferred to what document?

    a. ____

18. System owners and common control providers may decide, based on a system or organizational risk assessment, that certain findings are inconsequential and present what?

    a. ____

19. In all cases, organizations review assessor findings to determine what?

    a. ____

    b. ____

20. Senior leadership involvement in the mitigation process is necessary to ensure what?

      a. ____

          ____

      b. ____

          ____

21. What are some references for this task?

      a. ____

      b. ____

Notes:

____

____

____

____

____

____

____

____

____

____

____

____

____

____

____

Plan of Actions and Milestones

NIST SP 800-37, Task A-6

Acronyms

Define the following new acronyms

No new acronyms are defined in this task

Complete the following

1. What is the title of this task?

    a. ____

2. What are some potential inputs for this task?

    a. ____

    b. ____

    d. ____

    e. ____

3. What is the expected output from this task?

    a. ____

    b. ____

    c. ____

    d. ____

4. Who has primary responsibility for this task?

    a. ____

    b. ____

    c. ____

5. What roles support this task?

    a. ____

    b. ____

    c. ____

    d. ____

    e. ____

    f. ____

    g. ____

    h. ____

    i. ____

    j. ____

    k. ____

6. How does this task align with the SDLC?

    a. ____

    b. ____

    c. ____

7. How does this task align with the CSF?

    a. ____

8. The security and privacy assessment reports describe what?

    a. ____

    b. ____

9. If the AO decides that certain findings represent significant, unacceptable risk, what is required?

    a. ____

10. What should be done if an assessment finding can be quickly and easily remediated with existing resources?

    a. ____

11. The control reassessments determine what?

    a. ____

    ____

    ____

12. What do the assessors update with the findings from the reassessment?

    a. ____

13. When the control assessor updates the document in 12, do they change the original results?

    a. ____

14. At the completion of the control assessments what document(s) should be updated to reflect the accurate description of the implemented controls?

    a. ____

    b. ____

15. What does an addendum to the security and privacy assessment reports that provide?

    a. ____

    ____

16. Does the addendum does change or influence the initial assessor findings provided in the reports?

    a. ____

    ____

17. The issue resolution process can also ensure that only substantive items are identified and transferred to what document?

    a. ____

18. System owners and common control providers may decide, based on a system or organizational risk assessment, that certain findings are inconsequential and present what?

    a. ____

19. all cases, organizations review assessor findings to determine what?

    a. ____

    b. ____

20. Senior leadership involvement in the mitigation process is necessary to ensure what?

    a. ____

    ____

    b. ____

    ____

21. What are some references for this task?

    a. ____

    b. ____

Notes:

____

____

____

____

____

____

____

____

____

____

____

____

____

____

____

____

Authorization Package

NIST SP 800-37, Task R-1

Acronyms

Define the following new acronyms

No new acronyms are defined in this task

Complete the following

1. What is the title of this task?

    a. ____

2. What are some potential inputs for this task?

    a. ____

    b. ____

    c. ____

    d. ____

3. What is the expected output from this task?

    a. ____

    ____

    ____

4. Who has primary responsibility for this task?

    a. ____

    b. ____

    c. ____

5. What roles support this task?

    a. ____

    b. ____

    c. ____

    d. ____

6. How does this task align with the SDLC?

    a. ____

    b. ____

7. How does this task align with the CSF?

    a. ____

8. At a minimum what documents must be included in the authorization package?

    a. ____

    b. ____

    c. ____

    d. ____

9. Additional information can be included in the authorization package?

    a. ____

10. Providing timely updates to the plans, assessment reports, and plans of action and milestones on an ongoing basis supports what?

    a. ____

    b. ____

11. If the system contains PII, who reviews the authorization package prior to authorizing officials making risk determination and acceptance decisions?

    a. ____

12. The information in the authorization package is used by authorizing officials to make what?

    a. ____

13. When controls are implemented by an external provider what is made available by the provider?

    a. ____

14. How can the authorization package be made available to the authorizing official?

    a. ____

    b. ____

    c. ____

15. Information to be presented to the authorizing official in assessment reports is generated in the format and with the frequency determined by what?

    a. ____

    ____

16. The assessment reports presented to the authorizing official include information about deficiencies in what?

    a. ____

    b. ____

    c. ____

17. The authorization documents are updated at an organization-defined frequency using automated or manual processes in accordance with what?

    a. ____

18. What are some references for this task?

    a. ____

    b. ____

    c. ____

    d. ____

Notes:

____

____

____

____

____

____

____

____

____

____

____

____

____

Risk Analysis and Determination

NIST SP 800-37, Task R-2

Acronyms

Define the following new acronyms

No new acronyms are defined in this task

Complete the following

1. What is the title of this task?

    a. ____

2. What are some potential inputs for this task?

    a. ____

    b. ____

    c. ____

    d. ____

    e. ____

3. What is the expected output from this task?

    a. ____

4. Who has primary responsibility for this task?

    a. ____

    b. ____

5. What roles support this task?

    a. ____

    b. ____

    c. ____

    d. ____

6. How does this task align with the SDLC?

    a. ____

    b. ____

7. How does this task align with the CSF?

    a. ____

8. At a minimum what documents must be included in the authorization package?

    a. ____

    b. ____

    c. ____

    d. ____

9. Who analyzes the information in the authorization package provided by the control assessor, system owner, or common control provider, and finalizes the determination of risk?

    a. ____

    b. ____

10. Who does the person in 10 collaborate with in this analysis?

    a. ____

    b. ____

11. What may influence the risk analysis and determination?

    a. ____

12. Who may provide additional information to the authorizing official that is considered in the final determination of risk?

    a. ____

    b. ____

13. The authorizing official analyzes the information in the authorization package when doing what?

    a. ____

14. The AO analyzes what to determine the current security and privacy posture of the system?

a. ____

15. What are some references for this task?

a. ____

b. ____

c. ____

d. ____

e. ____

f. ____

Notes:

____

____

____

____

____

____

____

____

____

____

____

____

____

____

____

Risk Response

https://youtu.be/PITeULEaw0U
NIST SP 800-37, Task R-3

Acronyms

Define the following new acronyms

No new acronyms are defined in this task

Complete the following

1. What is the title of this task?

    a. ____

2. What are some potential inputs for this task?

    a. ____

    b. ____

    c. ____

3. What is the expected output from this task?

    a. ____

4. Who has primary responsibility for this task?

    a. ____

    b. ____

5. What roles support this task?

    a. ____

    b. ____

    c. ____

    d. ____

    e. ____

    f. ____

    g. ____

    h. ____

    i. ____

    j. ____

6. How does this task align with the SDLC?

    a. ____

    b.

____

7. How does this task align with the CSF?

    a. ____

8. After risk is analyzed and determined, what are two ways organizations can respond to risk?

    a. ____

    b. ____

9. What may be used to help determine the preferred course of action for the risk response?

    a. ____

    b. ____

10. The planned mitigation actions are included in and tracked using what document?

    a. ____

11. When conducting a reassessment, the assessors update the assessment reports. Do they delete the old information?

    a. ____

12. Who is the only person who can accept risk?

    a. ____

13. Decisions on the most appropriate course of action for responding to risk may include some form of what?

    a. ____

14. Organizations determine acceptable degrees of residual risk based on what?

    a. ____

15. What are some references for this task?

    a. ____

    b. ____

    c. ____

    d. ____

    e. ____

    f. ____

Notes:

____

____

____

____

____

____

____

____

____

____

____

____

____

____

____

Authorization Decision

NIST SP 800-37, Task R-4

Acronyms

Define the following new acronyms

No new acronyms are defined in this task

Complete the following

1. What is the title of this task?

   a. ____

2. What are some potential inputs for this task?

   a. ____

3. What is the expected output from this task?

   a. ____

   b. ____

   ____

4. Who has primary responsibility for this task?

   a. ____

5. What roles support this task?

   a. ____

   b. ____

   c. ____

   d. ____

   e. ____

   f. ____

6. How does this task align with the SDLC?

   a. ____

   b. ____

7. How does this task align with the CSF?

    a. ____

8. Can the explicit acceptance of risk be delegated?

    a. ____

9. The authorizing official issues an authorization decision for the system or for organization-designated common controls after reviewing what?

    a. ____

10. Who does the AO consult with prior to making the final authorization decision?

    a. ____

    b. ____

11. The authorization decisions for individual systems consider what?

    a. ____

    b. ____

    c. ____

12. The authorization decision is conveyed by the authorizing official to who?

    a. ____

    b. ____

    c. ____

13. What does the authorization decision also convey?

    a. ____

    b. ____

    c. ____

       ____

    d. ____

14. For systems, the authorization decision indicates to the system owner what?

    a. ____

    b. ____

    c. ____

    d. ____

15. For common controls, the authorization decision indicates to the common control provider and to the system owners of inheriting systems what?

    a. ____

    b. ____

16. The authorization termination date is established by the authorizing official, what does this date indicate?

    a. ____

17. Organizations may eliminate the authorization termination date in what case?

    a. ____

18. The authorization decision is included with the authorization package and is transmitted to who?

    a. ____

    b. ____

19. Upon receipt of the authorization decision and the authorization package, the system owner or common control provider acknowledges and implements what?

    a. ____

20. When the system is operating under ongoing authorization, the authorizing official continues to be responsible and accountable for what?

    a. ____

    ____

21. For ongoing authorization, the authorization frequency is specified in lieu of what?

    a. ____

22. The authorizing official reviews the information with the specific time-driven authorization frequency defined by what or who?

    a. ____

23. In continuous monitoring if the risk remains acceptable, the authorizing official does what?

    a. ____

24. In continuous monitoring if the risk is no longer acceptable, the authorizing official does what?

      a. ____

25. Who determines the level of formality in the process of communicating and acknowledging risk acceptance?

      a. ____

26. What provides additional guidance on authorization decisions, the types of authorizations, and the preparation of the authorization packages?

      a. ____

27. What are some references for this task?

      a. ____

      b. ____

Notes:

____

____

____

____

____

____

____

____

____

____

____

____

Authorization Reporting

NIST SP 800-37, Task R-5

Acronyms

Define the following new acronyms

No new acronyms are defined in this task

Complete the following

1. What is the title of this task?

    a. ____

2. What are some potential inputs for this task?

    a. ____

3. What is the expected output from this task?

    a. ____

    b. ____

4. Who has primary responsibility for this task?

    a. ____

    b. ____

5. What roles support this task?

    a. ____

    b. ____

    c. ____

    d. ____

    e. ____

    f. ____

6. How does this task align with the SDLC?

    a. ____

    b. ____

7. How does this task align with the CSF?

    a. ____

8. Authorizing officials report authorization decisions for systems and common controls to who?

    a. ____

9. Reporting occurs only in what situations?

    a. ____

____

10. Authorizing officials also report what (that represents a significant security or privacy risk)?

    a. ____

11. Authorization decisions may be tracked and reflected as part of what?

    a. ____

12. What are some references for this task?

    a. ____

    b. ____

    c. ____

Notes:

____

____

____

____

____

____

____

____

____

____

____

System and Environment Changes

Acronyms

Define the following new acronyms

No new acronyms are defined in this task

Complete the following

1. What is the title of this task?

    a. ____

2. What are some potential inputs for this task?

    a. ____

    b. ____

    c. ____

    d. ____

    e. ____

    f. ____

    g. ____

    h. ____

    i. ____

3. What is the expected output from this task?

    a. ____

    b. ____

    c. ____

4. Who has primary responsibility for this task?

    a. ____

    b. ____

    c. ____

    d. ____

5. What roles support this task?

    a. ____

    b. ____

    c. ____

    d. ____

    e. ____

    f. ____

    g. ____

6. How does this task align with the SDLC?

    a. ____

    b. ____

7. How does this task align with the CSF?

    a. ____

    b. ____

8. Systems and environments of operation are in a constant state of change with changes occurring in what elements?

    a. ____

    b. ____

    c. ____

9. Organizations establish what to support configuration and change management?

    a. ____

10. Common activities within organizations can cause changes to systems or the environments of operation and can have what?

    a. ____

11. Unauthorized changes may occur because of what?

    a. ____

    b. ____

12. Once the root cause of an unauthorized change (or an authorized change that impacts the privacy posture of the system) has been determined what should happen?

    a. ____

13. What are some references for this task?

    a. ____

    b. ____

    c. ____

    d. ____

Notes:

____

____

____

____

____

____

____

____

____

____

____

____

Ongoing Assessments

https://youtu.be/bjfE5D88TU8
NIST SP 800-37, Task M-2

Acronyms

Define the following new acronyms

No new acronyms are defined in this task

Complete the following

1. What is the title of this task?

    a. ____

2. What are some potential inputs for this task?

    a. ____

    b. ____

    c. ____

    d. ____

    e. ____

    f. ____

    g. ____

    h. ____

3. What is the expected output from this task?

    a. ____

4. Who has primary responsibility for this task?

    a. ____

5. What roles support this task?

    a. ____

    b. ____

    c. ____

    d. ____

    e. ____

    f. ____

    g. ____

    h. ____

6. How does this task align with the SDLC?

    a. ____

    b. ____

7. How does this task align with the CSF?

    a. ____

8. After an initial system or common control authorization, the organization assesses controls on what basis?

    a. ____

9. The monitoring frequency for each control is based on what?

    a. ____

10. Ongoing control assessment continues as the information generated as part of what process that is correlated, analyzed, and reported to senior leaders?

    a. ____

11. Assessor independence during continuous monitoring introduces what?

    a. ____

    ____

12. To satisfy the annual FISMA security assessment requirement, organizations can use assessment results from control assessments that occurred, what are some examples of these assessments?

    a. ____

    b. ____

    c. ____

13. Existing assessment results are reused consistent with what?

    a. ____

14. What are some references for this task?

    a. ____

    b. ____

    c. ____

    d. ____

Notes:

____

____

____

____

____

____

____

____

____

____

____

____

____

____

____

____

____

Ongoing Risk Response

NIST SP 800-37, Task M-3

Acronyms

Define the following new acronyms

No new acronyms are defined in this task

Complete the following

1. What is the title of this task?

   a. ____

2. What are some potential inputs for this task?

   a. ____

   b. ____

   c. ____

   d. ____

3. What is the expected output from this task?

   a. ____

   b. ____

4. Who has primary responsibility for this task?

   a. ____

   b. ____

   c. ____

5. What roles support this task?

    a. ____

    b. ____

    c. ____

    d. ____

    e. ____

    f. ____

    g. ____

    h. ____

    i. ____

    j. ____

    k. ____

6. How does this task align with the SDLC?

    a. ____

    b. ____

7. How does this task align with the CSF?

    a. ____

8. Assessment information produced by an assessor during continuous monitoring is provided to who?

    a. ____

    b. ____

9. Who determines the appropriate risk response to the assessment findings or approves responses proposed by the system owner and common control provider?

    a. ____

10. Who implements the appropriate risk response?

    a. ____

    b. ____

11. What guide and inform the decisions regarding ongoing risk response?

    a. ____

    b. ____

12. What must happen for controls that are modified, enhanced, or added as part of ongoing risk response?

    a. ____

    ____

    ____

13. What are some references for this task?

    a. ____

    b. ____

    c. ____

    d. ____

    e. ____

    f. ____

    g. ____

    h. ____

Notes:

____

____

____

____

____

____

____

____

____

____

____

____

____

Authorization Package Updates

Acronyms

Define the following new acronyms

No new acronyms are defined in this task

Complete the following

1. What is the title of this task?

    a. ____

2. What are some potential inputs for this task?

    a. ____

    b. ____

    c. ____

    d. ____

3. What is the expected output from this task?

    a. ____

    b. ____

    c. ____

    d. ____

4. Who has primary responsibility for this task?

    a. ____

    b. ____

5. What roles support this task?

    a. ____

    b. ____

    c. ____

    d. ____

    e. ____

6. How does this task align with the SDLC?

    a. ____

    b. ____

7. How does this task align with the CSF?

    a. ____

8. To Achieve Near Real-time Risk Management, The Organization Updates what documents on an ongoing basis (at a minimum)?

    a. ____

    b. ____

    c. ____

9. During this task what occurs with the POA&M?

    a. ____

    b. ____

    c. ____

10. The frequency of updates to risk management information is at the discretion of who?

    a. ____

    b. ____

    c. ____

11. Ready access to the current security and privacy posture supports what?

    a. ____

    b. ____

12. What is important to ensure does not happen when updating security and privacy plans, assessment reports, and plans of action and milestones?

    a. ____

    b. ____

13. Providing an effective method to track changes to systems through configuration management procedures is necessary for what?

    a. ____

    b. ____

    c. ____

14. What are some references for this task?

    a. ____

    b. ____

Notes:

____

____

____

____

____

____

____

____

____

____

____

____

____

____

____

____

____

Security and Privacy Reporting

NIST SP 800-37, Task M-5

Acronyms

Define the following new acronyms

No new acronyms are defined in this task

Complete the following

1. What is the title of this task?

    a. ____

2. What are some potential inputs for this task?

    a. ____

    b. ____

    c. ____

    d. ____

    e. ____

    f. ____

3. What is the expected output from this task?

    a. ____

4. Who has primary responsibility for this task?

    a. ____

    b. ____

    c. ____

    d. ____

5. What roles support this task?

    a. ____

    b. ____

6. How does this task align with the SDLC?

    a. ____

    b. ____

7. How does this task align with the CSF?

    a. ____

8. The results of monitoring activities are documented and reported to who?

    a. ____

    b. ____

9. Security and privacy posture reporting can be driven by what?

    a. ____

    b. ____

    c. ____

10. Rather, reporting is conducted in what manner?

    a. ____

11. The reports provide the authorizing official and other organizational officials with what type of information?

    a. ____

    ____

12. Security and privacy posture reports describe the ongoing monitoring activities employed by who?

    a. ____

    b. ____

13. What is the goal of the goal of security and privacy posture reports?

    a. ____

    ____

    ____

    ____

14. At a minimum, security and privacy posture reports summarize what?

    a. ____

    b. ____

    c. ____

15. The frequency of security and privacy posture reports is at the discretion of who?

    a. ____

16. Authorizing officials use the security and privacy posture reports to determine what?

    a. ____

17. Security and privacy posture reports are marked, protected, and handled in accordance with what?

    a. ____

18. What are some references for this task?

    a. ____

    b. ____

    c. ____

Notes:

____

____

____

____

____

____

____

____

____

____

____

____

____

____

Ongoing Authorization

NIST SP 800-37, Task M-6

Acronyms

Define the following new acronyms

No new acronyms are defined in this task

Complete the following

1. What is the title of this task?

    a. ____

2. What are some potential inputs for this task?

    a. ____

    b. ____

    c. ____

    d. ____

    e. ____

3. What is the expected output from this task?

    a. ____

    b. ____

    ____

    c. ____

    ____

4. Who has primary responsibility for this task?

    a. ____

5. What roles support this task?

    a. ____

    b. ____

    c. ____

    d. ____

    e. ____

    f. ____

6. How does this task align with the SDLC?

    a. ____

    b. ____

7. How does this task align with the CSF?

    a. ____

8. To employ an ongoing authorization approach organizations must have what in place?

    a. ____

    ____

9. Who reviews the security and privacy posture of the system on an ongoing basis to determine the current risk to organizational operations and assets, individuals, other organizations, and the nation?

    a. ____

    b. ____

10. The authorizing official may determine that the risk is no longer at an acceptable level for continued operation, and may issue what?

    a. ____

    b. ____

    c. ____

11. The authorizing official conveys updated risk determination and acceptance results to who?

    a. ____

    b. ____

12. The use of metrics and dashboards increases an organization's what?

    a. ____

13. What are some references for this task?

    a. ____

    b. ____

    c. ____

    d. ____

    e. ____

    f. ____

Notes:

____

____

____

____

____

____

____

____

____

____

____

____

____

____

____

____

____

____

System Disposal

NIST SP 800-37, Task M-7

Acronyms

Define the following new acronyms

No new acronyms are defined in this task

Complete the following

1. What is the title of this task?

    a. ____

2. What are some potential inputs for this task?

    a. ____

    b. ____

    c. ____

3. What is the expected output from this task?

    a. ____

    b. ____

    c. ____

4. Who has primary responsibility for this task?

    a. ____

5. What roles support this task?

    a. ____

    b. ____

    c. ____

    d. ____

    e. ____

    f. ____

6. How does this task align with the SDLC?

      a. ____

      b. ____

7. How does this task align with the CSF?

      a. ____

8. What are some examples of disposal controls?

      a. ____

      b. ____

      c. ____

      d. ____

9. Who should be notified of a system that is being disposed of?

      a. ____

10. What should be reviewed when a system is going through disposal?

      a. ____

11. Organizations removing a system from operation update what?

      a. ____

12. The use of metrics and dashboards increases an organization's what?

      a. ____

13. What are some references for this task?

      a. ____

      b. ____

      c. ____

Notes:

____

____

____

____

____

____

About The (ISC)² CAP

Exam Attempt Cost: $599 (USD)

Number of Questions: 125

Question Format: Multiple Questions

Exam Length: 3 Hours

Testing Center: Pearson VUE Testing Center

Domains

1. Information Security Risk Management Program (15%)
2. Categorization of Information Systems (IS) (13%)
3. Selection of Security Controls (13%)
4. Implementation of Security Controls (15%)
5. Assessment of Security Controls (14%)
6. Authorization of Information Systems (IS) (14%)
7. Continuous Monitoring (16%)

Experience Requirements

- Candidates are required to have two (2) years of cumulative work experience in at least one (1) of the seven (7) domains of the CAP common body of knowledge (CBK).

- If the candidate does not have the required experience, they will have three (3) years to gain the two years of required experience. Candidates that successfully pass the CAP but do not have the required experience will be an Associate of the (ISC)² until they possess the required experience.

www.ingramcontent.com/pod-product-compliance
Lightning Source LLC
Chambersburg PA
CBHW080736120726
48001CB00009B/2608